AMAZING AMPHIBIANS

TOADS

JAMES E. GERHOLDT

Published by Abdo & Daughters, 4940 Viking Drive, Suite 622, Edina, Minnesota 55435.

Library bound edition distributed by Rockbottom Books, Pentagon Tower, P.O. Box 36036, Minneapolis, Minnesota 55435.

Printed in the United States.

Cover Photo credit: Peter Arnold
Interior Photo credits: James Gerholdt
                Natural Selection pages 14, 20, 21
                Courtesy of Black Hills Reptile Gardens pages 6, 7, 16

Edited By Julie Berg

LIBRARY OF CONGRESS CATALOGING-IN-PUBLICATION DATA

Gerholdt, James E., 1943—
    Toads / James E. Gerholdt.
         p.   cm. -- (Amazing amphibians)
    Includes bibliographical refernces and index
    ISBN 1-56239-312-X
    1. Toads--Juvenile literature. [1. Toads.]
    I. Title. II. Series: Gerholdt, James E., 1943- Amazing amphibians.
    QL668.E227G47   1994
    597.8'7--dc20
                                 94-19202
                                 CIP
                                 AC

CONTENTS

TOADS

Toads are amphibians. Amphibians are ectothermic. This means they get their body temperature from the environment. Toads like it cool. If they get too hot, they will die. And if they are too cool, their bodies won't work. Toads need moisture to live, or they will dry up and die. But they do not need as much moisture as frogs do. There are almost 500 species of toads found in the world. They are found almost everywhere. Toads usually have bumpy skin and short legs. You cannot get warts from handling a toad!

You can see the bumpy skin and short legs on this American toad from Minnesota.

This toad is much lighter in color and blends in with its surroundings.

SIZES

Some toads grow to be very large. The Blomberg's and Rococo toads from South America can have a body over 8 inches long. The Colorado River toad from the United States and the Marine toad from South America both grow to about 6 inches in length. But most species are much smaller. The tiny Oak toad from the southeastern United States may be only 1 inch long! But most toads are from 2 to 4 inches in length.

The Marine toad from South America is one of the largest in the world.

The Colorado River toad from the southwestern United States grows to be very large.

SHAPES

Most toads are round and fat, with short legs. They can't jump, like a frog, but hop instead. Sometimes they will just walk! What makes a toad different from a frog is its skin. Toads have dry, bumpy skin. These bumps look like warts. Some toads do have smooth skin, but not many. Toads also have parotoid glands. These are large bumps, right behind the eyes that secrete bad-tasting poison. Some toads have shovels on their hind feet! These are called spadefoot toads. The Surinam toad from South America is very flat!

You can see the warts and the parotoid gland on this albino American toad.

This Southern toad from southeastern United States is walking.

COLORS

All toads have colors that help them blend in with their surroundings. This is called camouflage. Most toads are some shade of brown, but some have a lot of green. An example is the Green toad from Europe. Many species have attractive patterns and spots that make up for their plain colors. Some of the South American species have very bright colors. The fire-bellied toads from Europe and Asia are also brightly colored, with green on the back, and bright red or orange on the belly.

If you look closely, you will see a Red-spotted toad from Texas.

The Oriental Fire-bellied toad from Asia has bright colors.

HABITAT

Toads need moisture to live. But they don't need as much moisture as frogs. So, they are often found far from water. Sometimes you will find a toad in your garden. Some species live in the mountains while some live on prairies or even in deserts. Some, like the spadefoot toads, burrow into the ground and only come out if it rains. Sometimes they stay underground for several years. The Great Plains narrowmouth toad also lives in the desert and may share its burrow with a tarantula! The Surinam toad spends its entire life in the water.

This Marine toad from Texas is at home in the thorn brush desert.

The Couch's spadefoot toad from Texas only comes out of the ground when it rains.

SENSES

Toads have the same 5 senses as humans. Their eyesight is very good. It allows them to see their enemies before it is too late to get away. The eyes have special glands to keep them moist. And they have movable eyelids to protect them. At the tip of the nose is a blind spot. Toads have to turn their head to see in front of them. Their hearing is also good, which helps them find their mates.

The eye of this toad is large, giving it good eyesight.

This albino American toad has a blind spot directly in front of its nose.

DEFENSE

The most important defense of toads is their camouflage. But if their enemies see them they can't jump away like a frog or treefrog. They can only hop, and maybe escape to the safety of a pond. Toads defend themselves against their enemies by tasting bad! If an enemy grabs a toad in its mouth, it will drop it in a big hurry. Some species, like the Colorado River toad and the Marine toad, can actually kill an enemy with their bad taste. The bad tastes come from the parotiod glands behind the eyes.

The bad taste from the parotoid gland of this Marine toad can kill an enemy.

*Southern toads secrete a foul-tasting mucus
that scares away its enemies.*

FOOD

Toads will eat almost anything that moves and will fit into their mouths. They also eat other animals. These might be insects, spiders, slugs, worms, or small mammals. Many species enjoy crickets or mealworms. A hungry toad will stalk its meal, then flick out its tongue to grab it and pull it back into its mouth. The Surinam toad eats fish along with other animals that live in the water. But while the adults all eat other animals, the tadpoles eat algae and other plants found in the water.

This Southern toad has just grabbed a tasty king mealworm.

When a toad swallows, it squeezes its eyes down into its head.

BABIES

Almost all toads lay their eggs in the water. Depending on the species, there may be from 100 to 30,000 eggs. Then they hatch into tadpoles (polliwogs). After a few weeks to 2 months, these metamorph (change) into tiny toads and leave the water. The Midwife toad from Europe lays its eggs on land, and the male carries them and keeps them moist. When they are due to hatch, he puts them in shallow water. The Surinam toad carries her eggs in shallow pits on her back.

This tadpole will soon change into an adult toad.

*This male Great Plains toad is
calling to attract a female.*

GLOSSARY

Amphibians (am-FIB-e-ans) - Scaleless animals with backbones that need moisture to live.

Algae (AL-gee) - A plant without a stem that lives in the water.

Camouflage (CAM-o-flaj) - The ability to blend in with the surroundings.

Ectothermic (ek-to-THERM-ik) - Regulating body temperature from an outside source.

Environment (en-VI-ron-ment) - Surroundings an animal lives in.

Habitat (HAB-uh-tat) - An area an animal lives in.

Metamorph (MET-a-morf) - Change from a larval frog or toad.

Polliwog (POLL-ee-wog) - A larval frog or toad.

Tadpole (TAD-pole) - A larval frog or toad.

Index

About the Author

Jim Gerholdt has been studying reptiles and amphibians for more than 40 years. He has presented lectures and displays throughout the state of Minnesota for 9 years. He is a founding member of the Minnesota Herpetological Society and is active in conservation issues involving reptiles and amphibians in India and Aruba, as well as Minnesota.

Photo by Tim Judy